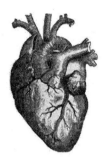

SEVENTY BEATS

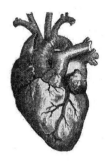

SEVENTY BEATS

Poems

by

Philippa Crundwell

THE KING'S ENGLAND PRESS

2015

ISBN 978 1 909548 46 6

SEVENTY BEATS

is typeset in

Doves Type, Book Antiqua and Gill Sans

and published by

The King's England Press

111 Meltham Road

Lockwood

HUDDERSFIELD

West Riding of Yorkshire

Printed and bound in Great Britain by

4Edge Ltd,

Hockley, Essex.

For my family,
the whole rowdy lot of you.

Contents

Being Human

For Our Eyes Only

These poems are for our eyes only;
Secrets between just you and me,
To reflect on when your heart is stony,
Or when your soul needs setting free,
If you read each word with thought and care,
And feel each beat from start to end,
Then I believe these words will take you somewhere,
You will feel the true message each nuance sends,
So please embrace them with devotion,
So you will connect with the narrative,
And imagine every depiction and notion,
That I, to you, took the time to give,
And remember these are secret words,
That may bring laughter, or reflection when lonely,
Or perhaps a new stance on events that occurred,
But remember - these are for our eyes only.

WORLD ISSUES

Peace One Day

When fragile words are spoken,
Then promises not kept,
Then someone may get broken,
And tears are often wept,
This is the massive void within,
The tender spot inside,
Where evil, hurtfulness and sin,
Have vandalised my pride,
So I set out to hurt you,
And cut you like a knife,
And after all you've been through,
I caused the deepest strife,
The gorge between us grew and grew,
So did those precious years,
Though neither of us ever knew,
We'd cried each other's tears,
I should have said I'm sorry,
So many years before,
Before we'd dug a quarry,
Between our bedroom doors,
I should have gently held your hand,
So many moons ago,
And tried to let you understand,
What I hope your heart might know,
I want to find a way to see,
Your side of the coin,
So I'll set my hate and anger free,
So that our hearts may join,
So can we cross the no-man's-land?
To iron out every crease,
So I can hold your tender hand,
And we can live in peace.

Defending Our Homeland

We are a forest of evergreen trees
In this war, this persecution
We are not felled by the breeze
We will stand side by side
At the border of our homeland
Where we'll take colossal pride
From defending the place we stand
For our roots are in the soil
That our ancestors have ploughed
And we won't let them destroy
This place and race of which we're proud
We'll sway our branches together
To the rhythm of the ancient earth
And take strength from the land
That gave our identity from birth
In this war, this persecution
They may attack us with their guns
But still we will stay standing
Even if some sap does run
And even if they fire our trunks
And we lay as ash and dirt
That's not the end; will never be
For we've left seeds in the earth
And we'll defend our homeland
And we surely will not die
Until there's no light from our sun
When the black clouds rule the sky.

When Society Takes Away Everything

Where is hope when society takes away everything?
But the skin on your bones
And your withered weary mind
Is there hope left in your heart?
When you are condemned
To a life sentence in a harsh, enclosed world
Where the ground is stubbornly hard with ice
In the skin-sizzling summer sun
When the wire fences wilt with heat
Is there hope left in your heart?
When you feel so afraid of that bullet
The one that is meant for you
Or of being tortured
Or worse
Hearing the screams of a loved one
In a cold, dark room
With small people
Revelling in the pain they cause
Is there hope left in your heart then?
Do you see the eagles flying?
Beyond the walls of guards
Beyond the metal fences
Above the pines on the mountain
And know somehow
That one day
You will reach that place again
Is there hope in your heart?
When you work the day through
Until your lungs can't take the dust
And you cough and cough
As if expelling
The hated thing inside you

And yet the eyes of those who keep you
Only brim with more hatred
And the mark of their stick on your skin
Agrees
Is there hope in your heart?
When more of those you know are brought in
To be resigned, confined, entwined
With the ways of 'life' that you must obey
There must be hope in your heart.
There is always
Always hope
Up until the moment you decide
(If you have the choice)
To end it all
There is a dying wail of hope
In the moment you pull the trigger
Or string the noose
There is a pious, pleading, pitiful hope
Even then
That there is a God
Or that there is not
There is hope for these things and more
You are brimming with hope at that moment
For something better
Beyond
Perhaps up in those snow-decorated mountains
That whisper with the clouds
And the sapphire sky
There is hope when society takes away everything
Otherwise there is nothing left
And you are not what you were
You are no longer human.

Merry War

Sword to sword in blood they'll brawl
To cross the enemy lines
Shattered with the pain they'll fall
For wars are merry times
Tooth for tooth, hand for hand
Gut for gut with bayonets
Sparring in the treacle land
Hopes of winning in straight sets
Deafened by the firing
Shaken stiff with strife
This harsh mental re-wiring
Stays with them all their life
In yellow poison they will drown
Singing songs of joy
To hide each tear and every frown
From their little boys
Muddied face and muddied heart
When it doesn't hurt to hurt another
See friends' corpses on a cart
Murder father, son and brother
They'll slash and crash and crumble
Have limbs blown off in mines
Get slaughtered if they stumble
For wars are merry times.

Subtle Reality

Sewn in amongst the fantasy
Is a strange subtle reality
Behind the guise of fairyland
A silent message underhand
Between the flakes of fairy dust
A spell of hate, or greed or lust
Is cast into this world of ours
Through fantasy's transcendent powers
Beneath each evil villain's cloak
A darker demon lurks in smoke
The talking clock that sings the time
Is there for reason not for rhyme
For pretext quite political
Or even darkly critical
May hide in every palace
Taint the wine in every chalice
For sewn in amongst the fantasy
Is a strange subtle reality
Beyond the make-believe's sweet looks
Is a truth that blends our world with books.

Hopeful but Alone

Said Abdul to Khaleid 'Merry Christmas Eve',
As he waited at the bus stop in the thickening mist,
How he had arrived here he couldn't conceive,
But he read the crumpled paper held tight in his fist.
The place to get a job was 'Lundon sity' he read,
As a tall man surveyed the unfamiliar child,
'Why are you here alone?' the Englishman said,
'I'm waiting for the bus... and Christmas.' He smiled.
'What do you want for Christmas?' asked the man: Mr. Cobb,
The boy whispered so quietly it could have been the wind,
'You want shelter, your family, as well as a job?'
Christmas brought Abdul hope so he nodded and grinned.
From the mist came the laugh of a jingling bell,
It was a laugh like Khaleid's before they bombed his home,
Soon the army had bombed Abdul's house as well,
So now Abdul was in England, hopeful but alone.
He looked up to see Mr. Cobb wasn't there,
Abdul started; he'd thought Cobb was catching the bus,
What did it matter? Why should he care?
He'd just vanished without a word or a fuss.
Then Abdul's forehead creased into a frown,
The man had seemed curious, yet pretentiously coy,
Khaleid had told him to keep his head down,
But he wasn't illegal, just an innocent boy.
A blue and neon car came from the misty night,
Purring towards him with purpose and speed,
Abdul wiped away the tears that impaired his sight,
'Merry Christmas from England' he whispered to Khaleid.

The Match of '89

The howling wind that never dies,
Soaring desperate screams and cries,
Of those who hurt and died alone,
Of those who didn't come back home,
'89 oh '89, the promises God broke that day
'89 oh '89, destroyed our hearts in every way,
They had to fight to breathe in pain,
The crowd of that now famous game,
It wasn't right; it wasn't sane,
For all it was: a match, a game,
'89 oh '89 an ugly blot on history's page,
'89 oh '89 the turmoil, the suffering, anger and rage,
The howling wind blows through the trees,
A gentle message rides the breeze,
Remember here two girls we lost,
The ticket with the dearest cost,
Remember now, their frightened eyes,
When you hear those roaring football cries,
And remember too, we vowed back then,
That history must not happen again.

Stop Thinking for the Holidays

Stop thinking about notoriety for the holidays
Find a peaceful place beside a silver stream
Settle in there amongst the heather and copious grass
Let yourself drift like the water's flow and dream
Stop thinking about criminality for the holidays
Lie down and watch the water stroke the stones
The dark back streets and tacky corner shops will wait
Whilst you sip the cool air and rest your bones
Stop thinking about disreputability for the holidays
Watch the clumsy lambs dancing on the hill
Shoot at the world with your camera this time
And listen to the blackbird's bold, handsome trill
Stop thinking about radicalism for the holidays
Freedom is everywhere, just look up to the sky
The world is beautiful by the stream in the hills
Watch the swallows soar and you'll understand why
Stop thinking about militancy for the holidays
Take off your sticky socks, cast them away
Paddle in the cold, silky, fresh flow of water
And you will feel the glory of a peaceful holiday.

Watch Your Step

A whispered rumour caught and bottled
can become a danger,
It can stretch, grow and turn slowly from question to
answer
Forever capturing a moment in time
with the wrong people can be terrible,
It might twist, turn and be tinkered with –
so people forever see it at the wrong angle
A message being recorded however subtle
could choke the world,
If it's replayed louder and louder every time
until the true meaning is irrelevant
A discreet gentle word over a shoulder
may become a roar of anger blasted across
A city,
A country,
Then the world
Anyone can be evil if they are shaped
and moulded into the right position,
And the mould blown up a thousand times
until it's the only thing you can see
An imprint on your retina
Feed a person a story, no matter how terrible,
They'll swallow it if it's shoved in their face
You have to watch your step being a celebrity;
Journalists have huge noses pearly with sweat,
lusting for a story
And even larger feet that have grown
way beyond their personal sphere
They set traps and tricks and lay ears in your path -
They'll trip you up eventually.

Elephant Song

At the watering hole there are musical cries,
Great fountains of water are sprayed at the skies,
Strong, charcoal bodies with dark wrinkled features,
These, surely, are Kenya's most beautiful creatures,
But a saddening blue are the notes that they sing,
For they know that their future's a vulnerable thing,
These creatures await a terrible fate,
As they bellow and bath and compete for a mate,
As you stalk them and watch them all mighty and wild,
Do you see them as money, not father and child?
Do you aim for his brains when you shoot through his
hide?
Does your small heart not ache for the calf at his side?
And when the brave creature cascades to his knees,
Do you know that your face is the last thing he sees?
Once you've run with your gun to the place where he fell,
Is that all you can think of - the goods that you'll sell,
Do you not hear his last trumpeting cry?
As the humble beast closes his dark eyes to die,
He's a grandiose giant you've known from the start,
So are his tusks truly worth more than his heart?
Yes, why do you poach when you know it's so wrong?
Do you not hear the great elephant's song?

Taken

Vision of the amber rising sun,
As eighteen daggers tread the earth,

Body of grass; of night and fire,
An elegant creature from her birth.

A ruby plucked out of a glittering crown,
Tranquillised, kidnapped, thrown in the back,
Driven away from her habitual forest,
They stole her mind to make her world black.

Glazed over eyes of misted up glass,
Unaware of events; unaware she's alone,
Taken far, far away to an alien place,
Stolen from family; stolen from home.

Locked up, confined, nowhere to run,
Eyeing her inmates with large dark jewels,
Pacing, pacing, pacing the cage,
The on-looking capturers sniggered, the fools.

Babies sprawled sticky fingers all over the glass
Parents came, and saw, and left, then forgot,
Children skipped by with an ignorant glance,
They let her heart die and her spirit rot.

From a...
Vision of the amber rising sun,
As eighteen daggers tread the earth,
Body of grass; of night and fire,
An elegant creature from her birth.

To a...
Vision of freedom and the wilderness,
Trapped in one room, with nothing to do,
Body of weakness, lost hope and desire,
An elegant tiger imprisoned in a zoo.

Poisoned Island

Island oh island do tell me your tale,
Why are there no chocolate ice creams for sale?
Why is there no trace of sand by your sea?
Why is this no place for people to be?
Where are your hotels and villas with pools?
Where are your rivers and blue waterfalls?
Where is your music so lively and free?
Oh why is this no place for people to be?
Was it us that stole it, dear island, you say?
But how did *we* take all your beauty away?
How did we wipe the palm trees from your shore?
What did we do and what could it be for?
Cartwheeling packets from sugary sweets,
Old ice cream wrappers from summer sun treats,
Oil barrels stacked up in brown plastic mountains,
Sulphur dioxide and CO_2 fountains,
Rubbish and litter line the shores of your sea,
Flies fill the air where the people should be,
A carcass of life as it was here before,
Before the pollution surrounded your shore,
Before the beer cans ran silvery streams,
Before the seabirds died in oil drowned dreams,
Before poisons and toxins soaked your gold sand,
Before this became the Maldives rubbish land,
Yes, this is no place for people to be,
In a plastic bag desert by the chemical sea,
You are the island that tourists avoid,
Because this is the landscape that humans destroyed.

Fragile Earth

Who cares for the earth's fragility?
It's human's responsibility
But now it seems that nobody cares
For the birds, antelopes and grizzly bears
And we've scraped coloured coral off the sea floor
As over-fishing continues to soar
And our need to build houses, roads and train stations
Has led to some drastic deforestation
Yes, the deforestation (we've caused that as well)
How long left for the Amazon? No-one can tell
So the rivers of sewage are the least of our troubles
As they drain to the seas of yellow-brown bubbles
And those fresh water creatures that are found dead
Due to the toxins and poisons we've spread
And poaching rare creatures for their teeth, tusks or skin
Is still carried out (though considered a sin)
And though animal activists holler and shout
Siberian tigers are still dying out
And these terrible bombs that we want to release
Ruin the land and shatter the peace
And the litter that foams like a fierce tidal wave
Buries our streets in a sweet-wrapper grave
An army of automobiles, boats and trains
Cause torrents of fumes like roaring jet planes
So who cares for the earth's fragility?
It's human's responsibility
But I saw a picture online yesterday
Where a diver encounters a Great White in the bay

And it said in the text "This animal here,
Is the most dangerous creature ever, we fear"
And suddenly the message became quite clear,
As it said "He kills millions every year"
Every action that harms our world - we must ban it
So we can save our small, fragile planet.

Changing City

A hectic hub of humanity,
Joy, sadness, anger, strife,
A shaken lemonade can,
Just fizzing full of life,

But the busy city changes,
With the setting seaside sun,
When nightclubs start invading,
Enslaving city young,

A concentration of creation,
Where graffiti art is thick,
By night, a spreading web of words,
Engulfing every brick,

Booze and blaring music,
And careless screeching cries,
Between the breaths of cigarettes,
Fill troubled, smoky skies,

Shattered glass shop windows,
Fragmented works of art,
Glinting in the moonlight,
Piercing through my heart,

Stop the changing city,
Splitting at the seams,
In the cloak of darkness,
In alcoholic dreams,

Stop the changing city,
Turning now to sin,
Torn at from the outside,
But hurting from within.

One-Souled World

I've a hope and dream of time and place,
When we share one soul: the human race,
A place and time where duchess and beggar,
Are as equal as Saint Agur blue and plain cheddar,
When the rich and the posh folk don't pass the poor by,
Or strut with their nose in the air quite so high,
When they don't screw it up
like they've smelt something vile,
They instead drop a copper or a warm welcome smile,
When the callous remarks about class are not there,
Then I know we've arrived at a world that is fair,
And the cost of your skirt or your Au de Jai vest,
Are not the way that we judge who's the best,
Or the size of your house or your dog or your nails,
Are not the reasons one passes or fails,
Instead it's the love and the care that you show,
Not the places you've been or the people you know,
I've a hope and dream of time and place,
When we share one soul: the human race.

Beyond this Earth

If you believe what I believe
Another world you could conceive
Another life beyond this earth
Free from harness, chains and girth
Beyond our milky tear-streaked skies
Past our silent moon's grey eyes
Yonder our sun's flames and fire
A place whose beauty will inspire
If you believe what I believe
Another world you could conceive
A land with resource to sustain
A place with space to entertain
An earth without a room of faces
Dictating - segregating races
A land where not a single life
Need take another to survive
Or rip a life away with choice
Or harm another to rejoice
If you believe what I believe
Another world you could conceive
But could not reach for distance and time
Are the difference between reason and rhyme.

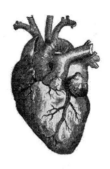

PLACES ON THE PLANET

Paradox Landscape

The roughly cut cliffs crumble into the sea,
Like tumbling sand from a sandcastle wall,
The whispering grass creeps up to the edge,
Of the deadly plunge down to the cold sapphire pool,
The dusty gold path that winds down to the beach,
Is lined with red butterflies - bright in the sun,
And the heather grows pungent in the shimmering heat,
As the darkening sand and the sea become one,
The endless blue sphere caresses the coast,
The soft arch of the sand reflecting our lips,
The shiny white teeth like the dazzling grains,
And the ends of the line curled up at the tips,
Each rippling wave is a smooth rolling swell,
As it smashes the sand with the beat of a drum,
The old gnarled trees are bent in the breeze,
Where the yarrow plants dance and the bumblebees hum,
The roughly cut cliffs crumble into the sea,
Like tumbling sand from a sandcastle wall,
Paradox landscape of waves, sand and scree,
When the beautiful sea makes the cliffs slowly fall.

Painted Mountains

Candyfloss clusters floating by,
In the cornflower ocean sky,
Above a sea of vivid green,
Silent, snowdropped and serene,
In a pale grey monster's lap,
Drizzled with white icing cap,
Upon the sloping mountain side,
A smudge of snow some miles wide,
Peppered with strong earthy pines,
Ringing with sweet cowbell chimes,
Springs are springing fresh and cool,
Which seep into a mountain pool,
In the gorge a chalet rests,
A speck beneath the rising crests,
Which rule the world where eagles fly,
In the cornflower ocean sky.

Heaven's Tears

When dear heaven wants to cry,
A billion drops fall from the sky,
And although the golden sun has fought her,
To spare the earth from all the water,
Sweet heaven knows that she must cry,
To stop the earth from turning dry,
She pelts the earth with jewels so sad,
She knows the people will feel glad,

When bloom the ripe fruit and the grain,
Because of heaven's silver rain,
And when the gold sun's full and proud,
When radiance breaks through the cloud,
And without the rain they wouldn't know,
How glorious the sun's warm glow.

Valley of Storms

Rest here in the silent land,
Under dregs of storms above,
Majestic hills and mountains stand,
Peaceful as a ghostly dove,
Rained heaven's hands are slowly forging,
Chiselled valleys through the rock,
Emerald gullies, gushing, gouging,
With the ticking of a soundless clock,
Whispered gasps of secret word,
Stolen from the mountain peak,
By he who know not what he heard,
Just whips away each breath you speak,
Dilapidated farmhouse shells,
Rooftops ripped away by he,
Join the icy ocean swells,
As cliff tops crumble to the sea,
Rest here in the silent land,
Where tears will sing and souls will burn,
Majestic hills and mountains stand,
In the land where storms return.

Seasons' Rain

The rain's here again
Drizzly and blinding
The dusk grey clouds
Have split their binding
Sour with each sorrow
Of the winter's freeze
Carried in swiftly
On the bitter breeze
But the wind will whip
Away that rain
Blow away the grief
The frosty pain
So the new rain sings
With soft fat notes
On each spring leaf
She plops pearl coats
Gives life to plants
A gleam to the lawn
And quenches the thirst
Of new animals born
She cleanses the pores
Of a human face
Soaks their tongue buds
With a fresh earthy taste
Then the rain is condensed
To a thick summer storm
Each bead saturating
Sweet smelling and warm
It draws life outdoors
To witness the sight
Of the gold-purple drops
Turning grain and fruit ripe

Then the sun hides away
Autumn showers appear
A mouldering mixture
Of rain from the year
It forms grey-green puddles
And clings to the leaves
Tweezing and pulling
Red stars from the trees
Then on the bed
Of soft golden hues
She pours on old treasures
From birches and yews
Until one cold evening
She arrives here again
Sheets of blinding
Winter rain.

Above Me

A vast scrapbook sky,
Stretched above the rooftops,
Washed in cornflower ink,
Clumped with cotton wool,
Sighs with breathless purity,
Smiles with ingenuity,
Displays itself above me,
A picture I could never paint,
A silver mountain high,
Above my insignificance,
Shadowing my brevity,
Laughs at my flare of life,
A hurricane's wise eye,
Stares down at me in peace,
Whilst her red-brown arms,

Rip my fragile world away,
The coal-black wash of dye,
That smothers neon nights,
Allows white stars and planets,
To mock the lights of Earth,
The earth won't tell us why,
Nature lets us be,
Then whips up a stormy sea,
She uproots an ancient tree,
And unleashes thunder free,
It's all above me.

Golden Days

Are you more than a summer's breeze?
Like hunting lions we chase your scent
Across vast lands and overseas
A dream to which our minds are bent
Are you comfort or deep desire?
Like cubs we tear at and savour your meat
We glimpse the divine or something higher
On those blue days of your gentle heat
Are you merely a golden glow?
Like withered donkeys we complain
When your glory turns to go
And again we see the face of rain
Are you more than a summer's breeze?
That elated joy of a smiling day
Those times we dearly hope to seize
But like treasured gold will hide away.

Blind in the Chase

He never noticed how beautiful, vast and stunning,
The hills looked so rich beneath the pale moon,
He chased the chalky path as he was running,
The wind whispered his pursuers were coming soon.

He'd never heard the rustles, the whispers, the whistles,
Never listened to the purr of the nightjar call,
He ran past the alder trees that mutter to the thistles,
Only at the old signpost did he dare to stall.

Brighton to the left or Keymer to the right,
Instead he ran on down the dale in-between,
To the eerie trees where he was out of sight,
But the barren wilderness didn't let him stay unseen.

He hid from the peeking sun that set alight the hillside,
He didn't hear the songbird with her gorgeous Irish lilt,
He shut himself off, for he was too preoccupied,
To look at the countryside's lovely patchwork quilt.

He never saw the picturesque toy houses far below,
He stumbled on a rock and rolled down the hill,
But still he did not smell the flowers sweetly grow,
He just ran through the morning, disturbing the still.

He dashed without senses, he shut tight his eyes
And stayed in his world filled with blacks, greys and browns
Did he know what he was missing - would he ever realize?
That he had never seen the beautiful South Downs.

Night Time on the Lake

The wind ripples through my cotton shirt
As I sit alone on the lake
I embrace the silence around me
As I sit and contemplate
I dream of a perfect future
Under the smoky moon
A rowing boat away from truth
No need to go home soon
Water and sky - blue mirrors of each other
Yet the trees are black upon the shore
The air is fresh
My lungs crave more
A round swell forms on the water's surface
A glimpse of yellow eye
But I left my hooks on the shore tonight
I'll say the fish were shy
Then the water is tranquil beneath me
As silent and still as I
And I smile here in my night-time world
Of silver lake and sky.

Land of Lost Gifts

Here is the dumping land
Of those never-worn woollies
You can't sell second hand
Here is the bizarre bazaar
A messy hostel for teapots
Slippers and antique guitars
Here help the frumpy cavaliers
That posse of local do-gooders,
Duke of Edinburgh volunteers
Here wait the needles of treasures lost
In a haystack of clutter they hide
The jewels some fool has tossed
Here assist the cancer fighters
And the hospice helpers
The age-concerned and wrong-righters
Here hang the clothes of pungent scent
Of memories or somewhere else
Not washed before they went
Here is the mystique land
Of foreign silks, exotic tops
Of strange, aromatic, charismatic things
Here inside this charity shop.

My Flock of Silver Arrows

I see the geese of moonlit skies,
A train of long-necked sparrows,
Croaking, rasping, honking cries,
My flock of silver arrows,
The white suns hang there, burning bright;
The day is not yet dawning,
"So take the next star to the right,
And head straight on 'til morning,"
The arrows' wings beat like my heart,
Their voice as hoarse as mine,
Their strong formations never part,
Or feathers cease to shine,
And up above, far, far away,
A soft lute and a lyre,
Strum the night through to the day,
With heaven's angel choir,
And as the clouds now cross the moon,
And hide the night's parade,
The stars creep back into the gloom,
My silver arrows fade.

Mist-Kissed Morning

On the slick shining grass silver with dew
I stand in my socks with the damp soaking through
And there on the wall between Alfie's and mine
A charcoal bird trills in the morning's sunshine
His feathers as fluffy as freshly turned soil
His eyes are a rainbow of sun on spilt oil
As crisp clean and clear as a piper he plays
His beak is an ember in the golden sun's rays
On thin twigs he bobs like a proud clockwork toy
Puffing his chest out and trilling for joy
Then he springs from the wall in a flurrying flight
Hops onto the grass iridescent with light
Where he prances and stamps with his limbs tied to strings
And marches and jumps in a frolic of wings
And there on that spot where his feet softly pound
An indignant pink noodle he plucks from the ground
Then the still wind rears up and tugs at my hair
And the sun paints a glittering mist everywhere
And my blackbird takes flight to the icy blue skies
And I see myself now in my small blackbird's eyes
A pale creature alone and estranged on the lawn
In this wintery garden caressed by the dawn
On this slick shining grass golden with dew
I stand proud in my nightgown and admire the view.

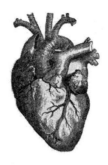

SOME
NOT-SO-SERIOUS
POETRY

Grumbling Granny

My knitting's in a pickle and the pickle's mixed with jam,
My laundry's in a jumble and the mouse is in the flan,
My curlers aren't a-curlin'; they're rolling down the lane,
My rocking chair's been broken and the bear's a stonkin' pain,
He's shredded all the wallpaper, he's smashed my vase apart,
The quack is coming, running for my irregular beating heart,
My bookshelf is collapsing upon my wine glass case,
The dog is dashing round the house
In a great destruction race,
My flowers are uprooted, the bird table's knocked down,
My legs are creaking and a-groanin' so I can't go into town,
My prize collection of thimbles is rolling round the floor,
And Geraldine, the ill-mannered goat,
is kicking down the door,
The teapot's far from cosy, as it's sitting in the tea,
The fox has got my knitting…argh! I just can't bear to see!
The stoat ate up my garters and is nibbling my slippers,
Geraldine's munching at the bread,
Now she's swallowed the nail clippers!
The monkey chopped the curtains to brew up in his stew,
Why do the kids treat their granny like this?
I don't know what to do!

Christmas at Granny's

Bernie's father went to jail
When Bernie's mother went away
So Bernie's Granny had to keep
Bernie for the holiday
Christmas is the time of year

- It might be worth recapping -
That kids like Bernie want to have
Surprises in red wrapping
But Granny knew not what to do
Of course she'd lived a thousand years
But buying gifts for children was
One of her greatest lifelong fears
Now that old Granddad had passed
- He used to buy for Bernie's Dad -
She had no-one to shop for her
So things were looking pretty bad
"I'm thrilled, Granny!" young Bernie yelled
- She was an optimistic child -
"Santa will bring lots of toys;
There's space for them to all be piled."
"Now Bernie, dear," old Granny sighed
"What is it that you'd like?"
"I'd make a list, but Santa knows!"
Squealed Bernie in delight
It was the morn of Christmas Eve
So Granny vowed to do her shop
But Bernie caught her at the door
And cried "You can't leave in that top"
So Granny stayed at home that morn
Displayed each garment on the floor
Until she had approval that
She could (with style) walk out the door
'Twas not until late afternoon
That Granny reached the little town
Where half the shops had closed early
And half the shops had been shut down
So Granny sadly traipsed back home
With empty bags and spirits low
Poor Bernie would have nothing now

It wasn't even going to snow
But would old Granny just give up
And go to bed on Christmas Eve
Knowing that wee Bernie would
Have not one present to receive?
Then Granny had a brainwave
She'd call her brother Sam
Who had his grandkids over
But lived in Birmingham
"Sammy, Sammy, do come stay"
Begged Granny down the phone,
"You can barely tell it's Christmas
In my dark and dismal home"
And with giggling and muttering
It was lastly agreed
That Sam would come with family
Surprises guaranteed
So early Christmas morning
Bernie jumped on Granny's bed
And screamed so loud it could be heard
By all alive and dead
"There are elves in the hall, Granny
There are elves in the bath
And best of all - you won't believe…
SANTA'S in the hearth!"
"That's lovely Bernie, dear, smiled Gran
Glad she'd hit a winner
"How many of them are there, Bern?
They're staying for Christmas dinner!"
When Granny reached the living room
She rubbed her sleepy eyes;
A giant tree was standing there
A beautiful surprise
And one could barely see the floor

For presents lined the room
And twenty elves were jigging
To a jolly Christmas tune
And Santa by the fireplace
Red coat and facial hair
Chuckled at young Bernie
Who just couldn't help but stare
"I told you Granny!" Bernie cried
"I believed you Bernie, child"
And Santa shot a wink at Gran
And Granny simply smiled.

Violet the Ghost

Shrouded in a thick darkness,
A chill seeping under the door,
Moths slowly die in the flickering flame,
Bones, ash and dust line the floor,
The darkness now seems to come closer,
A light scratching sounds at the door,
Heart thumping 'What is it'; 'Who is it'?
A chilling moan freezes your core,
The voice of a child sweetly singing,
The soft music floats through the door,
It sounds like the voice of Violet White-Sheet,
But you know Violet died years before,
The chair starts creaking behind you,
The light wavers under the door,
You turn your head to a strange growling sound,
Violet's preparing to roar
She's as small as the child you remember,
But slowly you edge to the door,
For her mouth is sprouting sabre sized teeth

Her hands are scaled; like pigeon claws,
The child's turning into a dragon
'That's not ghost-kids' normal pursuit!'
Perhaps this is only a film or a dream
Otherwise it's her new dragon-suit?

Old Uncle Ronny

Our uncle Ronny was a mad old fool
Lived in a lavatory cubicle
He drank from the cistern and he washed in the sink
And when he got some money he would spend it on drink
Wild as a stallion, drunk as a mule
He'd burn like wet petrol on his frothy brown fuel
And when they locked the gents up at the falling of night
Old uncle Ronny would be hiding out of sight
In his dirty grey prison he would dance to the tune
Of the dead black silence and the pale cold moon
And the townsfolk, years later, said something wasn't right
With the mad-man in the toilets swaying 'til the morning light
But our uncle Ronny was a happy old fool
He never earned a living and he never went to school
But he was mad and merry and that's more than can be said
For the rest of Old Branchester, who, at night, went off to bed.

La Fiesta de los Peces

Al lado del río hay la fiesta de los peces,
Siempre tiene baile y el flamenco a veces,
Y cuando escucho el ritmo de tambor,
Sé que van a abrir unas botellas de licor,
Porque a los peces (todos sabemos) les gusta tener -
Un buen tiempo hasta que se van a caer,
Con un tiburón piñata para romper,
Y una gran cantidad de vino para beber,
Los peces saben cómo hacer una buena diversión,
Siempre hay risa y mucha emoción,
Sus escamas brillan en la luz de la luna,
Para esta 'enfermedad fiesta' no hay una vacuna,
Las ratas de agua no pueden dormir cercana,
Por lo que emigran como la gitana,
Los peces dominan el río durante estas fiestas,
Creo que son hilarantes- no me molesta,
También me encanta verlos haciendo el tango,
O girar en sus colas- bailando el fandango,
Si bajan al río en una noche con la luna,
Podrán ver esta maravilla si tienen la buena fortuna.

Love from Procrastination

Procrastinate, procrastinate
Try to put off that 'due by' date
Go and do everything under the sun
Except that thing that ought to be done
Procrastinate, procrastinate
Leave that task until too late
Evade and shirk just to delay
That misty, hazy deadline day
Procrastinate, procrastinate
Create some reasons you should wait
To do that important or difficult deed
With pressure to do well or to succeed
Procrastinate, procrastinate
Do your jobs at a slower rate
Perfectionists you are my prey
Join the procrastinating way
Procrastinate, procrastinate
Rush at the end in a frantic state
Prolong and stretch that hesitation
My victims of procrastination!

In Our New Blue Yacht

We were sailing on the sea
In our new blue yacht
Bare legs over the side;
The sun was young and hot
We weren't far from the beach
Filled with human sardines
We sneered at them
As we licked our ice creams
We were sailing on the sea
In our new blue yacht
Riding on the waves
In a picturesque spot
We squinted all around
To survey the scene
Surveying our surveyors;
We desired to be seen
We were posing on the sea
In our new blue yacht
Flashing diamonds on our fingers
Downing alcoholic shots
We giggled and we drank
And we drank and drank some more
Until became a blur
The shimmering shore
We were rolling on the decks
In our new blue yacht
Feeling rather tipsy
And beetroot-red-hot
We could see the beach
Filled with human sardines
They laughed at us
And we knew we'd been seen.

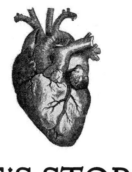

PEOPLE'S STORIES

The Child behind the Stair Gate

I always see that child behind the stair gate
In my mind's eye
When I remember the pain of being trapped
From the purple London rain
That sung colours in neon lights
That my fingers were numb for
From tugging at that lock
When father's back was turned
Which it always was (to my emotions)
But "Father was my protector?"
The child was an emaciated shadow
With an obtusely bright and fizzing mind
Full of worldly dreams
Of resplendent shops and bustling theatres
Yet living in a smog-festering grotto
Her gaunt face grew pale with longing
Naïve heart ever throbbing
With stings of his cruel words that ring in her mind
But that silence rings louder
From when she was left behind
I always see that child behind the stair gate
Yearning for love
To be free from grey bars
Excluding her from reality
From the cool, rainy London air
From the mother she did not see
But never knew why
I can feel the scars that burn with 'why?'
The scars of the child behind the stair gate
The grey wrinkles in my skin
Where the damage never healed
And now

I become that child again
In the purple London rain
I spin around in the dazzling city
I hear the scars in my voice
Absorbing every raindrop I laugh
And tremors in my foetus form
Embrace the warm current of bodies under umbrellas
I feel my cheeks pressing the bars
And I see the iridescent city lights dance
And slight arms stretching through the bars
I skip along in the glittering puddles
Arms longing to touch the purple sky-drops
That still fall all these years later
To remind me
Of my father's scorning eyes
That watched me, always
When I was trapped
A frightened child
And the acid factory-rain
Beautiful purple rain
Father's acid eyes
Scald my scars
Sings on my skin
To tell me
The child behind the stair gate
This woman
Will never be free.

The Dance of the Starlings

It was the last thing I saw for a very long time
Their last dance for me in the dying sunshine
How they soared and they swirled in the soft amber sun
Until their black bodies flew together as one
I stood in the field with the prison nearby
As they formed a dark storm in the cold, angry sky
They flew to the music of the swift, silent wind
Their cloud pierced my heart and I knew I had sinned
If they flew in those fields with every night past
Why did I only look during my last?
And why did I only see how the sun burned
In the last sunset before my key turned?
Silhouettes in the sky above the whispering trees
And the fiery red light and the icy cold breeze
And my bitter dry lips felt the rain from the skies
For the first time in years there were tears in my eyes
It was then that I knew why my life changed forever
For I'd fought the flock, but the birds worked together
I fell to my knees, raised my hands to the air
And my mouth screamed a fierce and fathomless prayer
Then the flock was a wave gripping the sea
The flock could be anything; they could fly free
And now all these years later with no second chance
The only beauty I know is the Starlings' last dance.

The Last Fledgling

A fumbling frolic of feathers and fluff,
And I'm perched on the brink of a wild new world,
My siblings were made of far braver stuff,
But I nervously get my small wings unfurled,
I gaze at the canopy rising above,
And hope with each beat of my pulsating heart,
That I can soar up, and fly like a dove,
And in this huge world I can make a great start,
They flutter and fly so free in the clearing,
But I'm left indecisive, panicked and scared,
Is it the stoats or the weasels I'm fearing?
Or is it the owls with their long talons bared?
Then I sight a familiar face,
Her majestic plumage is saffron and coal,
As she sings and her musical trills fill the space,
Like a mother horse calling her bandy legged foal,
I do long to hunt the way my mother hunts,
I long to sing the way my mother sings,
I am a great great tit, I'm not just the runt,
So bravely I leap as I spread my small wings.

City Park Dreams

I dreamed for a long while,
Of a face, albeit hazed,
That seemed to share your smile,
And looked a lot like yours,
As I sat on the wet bench,
In the fading city park,
I raised my eyes to the trees,
That grew human in the dark,
And blew a swirl of ghostly smoke,
From my bitter tasting lips,
That I realised had not spoke
Since we'd met two days ago.
In this self-same city park,
Along the path we'd walked,
Then across the grass we'd wandered,
It seemed a short time that we'd talked.
And now my skin grows wet,
From the damp that's soaking through,
These old jeans that I wore,
That one time I met you.
And I stand up now, upon the bench,
And stare up at the firmament,
I vow I see your face up there,
Drawn in the stars that heaven sent,
Could this mean that we will meet again?
In this very park, in a day or two,
Or do these stars say something else?
Do they tell me that you've joined them too?
I dare not dwell on this grim thought,
Instead I turn to wander home,
And everywhere, your face I sought,
Under each night-blacked hood.

And wandering between the grey tower-blocks,
That were the home of strangers yet,
It dawned that there were millions,
Of faces I had not yet met.
And I dreamed after I had left the park,
Of a vision of your face,
That looks different now in the dark,
As it smiles down at me from space.

Tarnished with Vengeance

Your lips frothing black
Overflowing with mirth
Blue-rope-veined claws
Pressed me hard on the earth
I hated, I loathed,
I defied with my eyes
But your flames of sweet fury
Silenced my cries
Silenced my red lips
Silenced normality
You returned me my body
But stole faith in humanity
And still the pain screams
And the scars shout red-raw
When you rip at fresh sleep
With your smiling blue claws
I will never forget
I will not cease my fears
Or find hope in a Bible
So flooded with tears
My lips frothing black
Overflowing with spite

My tarnished soul's restless
With vengeance each night
I hated, I loathed
I defied with my eyes
And now I shan't sleep
Until your conscience cries.

When You Were Here

Here is where I am and wherever I go,
And when you were Here I wanted you to know,
That I'd like you to stay – Here - with me,
But I couldn't say that to you, you see,
Because somehow I needed to know,
That you, to Here, wanted to go,
When you were Here I felt at ease,
With myself I felt somehow appeased,
Was it your eyes or was it your smile?
All I know is I wanted you to stay for a while,
There was something in your manner uncommon to find,
A warmth emanated and in your eyes a fun shined,
When you were Here something changed within me,
When you were Here my soul was set free,
And although Here is Here and where I go to,
I know Here is a place best shared with you.

Blessed with Forgiveness

I dug the sweet earth by the church
With the spade that had belonged to John
As I flung the fresh black soil behind
I heard the blackbird's merry song
The smile that tingled in my heart
Was evident upon my face
And with John's coffin by my side
It must have looked so out of place
Yet the song's notes rang with memories
Of striding through wild fields with John
Of kissing in the fresh spring breeze
Knowing where our hearts belonged
'Murder' rustles the autumn leaves
Muttered in clusters of floating crowds
Puzzled, judging, prying eyes
Pierced like sunlight through the clouds
For they can't understand my peace
They don't know how I can forgive
The man who killed John in cold blood
The man who took John's life, but lived
I lean upon John's trusty spade
Look up at the church with smiling eyes
John would want to cease my pain
With forgiveness, I have realised.

Lime-Green Moon

The moon was a pale lime-green last night
A ripe fruit severed, showing craters deep
She let her eerie, sickly light
Shine upon our blackened street
And we saw the craters here too, on Earth
Or on whichever planet we then were stood
They pooled the street like tears of foul mirth
Scarring and blemishing all that was good
I lied back then, to you, dear one,
As we dug through ash in that laughing mouth
I said the people must have gone
Like white winged birds to the beautiful south
"Beauty!" I spit the word; it's a lie
It hurts to say it - like blood from burst lungs
And you remember we heard that plaintive cry
As a child reached up for Heaven's rungs
I believe that cry will hurt most of all
If we survive these lime-green days
I will always think of that plaintive call
I could have gone to answer, but chose to stay
I chose to stay here with you, dear one
Under the moon of ugly lime-green
And I'll try not to wish that we too were gone
That we'd never been forced to see this dark scene
I do not believe that we'll ever recover
I do not believe so I no longer pray
I don't believe any more, but you're still my brother
You hold on to hope; and for this I will stay.

In the Park after Dark

My fingers are flighty fleas leaping
As I type this text on my phone
The people departed here hours ago
Now the sun too has left me alone
But that's not quite true something tells me
I'm not quite alone in the dark
You too are out there, near, somewhere
Alone tonight in the park
I hear the low noise I've awaited
In the trees a barn owl takes flight
I set off into the depths of the park
Into the quiet, lonely night
I see your hunched shape on a bench
I slow my fast pace to a walk
A feral cat slinks in the shadows
What is the prey that she stalks?
You arise and scan your surroundings
But I linger, masked by the trees
I recognise the light of your phone
And smell your strong scent on the breeze
You've seen me and start to approach me
Like two creatures at night in the park
Slowly we meet, estranged, yet so close
I reach out to you in the dark.

River of Dreams

Do you remember our dream river that night?
Do you still dream it, or is it out of sight?
Have our river dreams gone down that waterfall?
Do you still imagine it? Or can't you recall?
Has our dream river dried with every year past?
Did we dig the bed too deep? Let it flow too fast?
Do you remember our dream river that night?
Do you still hope for it with all of your might?
We said we'd row away in our boat for two
And journey to places exciting and new
Have our river dreams flowed into the sea?
To join every other dream never to be
Do you remember those dream nights at all?
Before they tumbled down that dark waterfall?
Is this land a desert, as dry as it seems?
Or do you still wish for our river of dreams?

New Year

This year will be different
Won't be like the last
Not by my doing
It won't go so fast
The way you decided
To leave me so soon
Some strings have been broken
Don't play the same tune
New Year's resolution
Make things work on my own
Been given no choice

But to live here alone
New Year's resolution
Sing a lonely girl's song
Can't resolve to be happy
Not with you gone
This year you won't be there
I'll work things out with just me
We were never caged in
But you set yourself free
You were my happiness
You were the cause
Yes, you were my New Year
But I wasn't yours.

Dusty Old Friend

If you hold me right I will breathe
And I will let you smell how musty
I have become through these centuries
If you trace your hands along my wrinkles
I will let you touch and feel how dusty
I have become through these centuries
If you dig your nails into my spine
I will let you hear how crusty
I have grown to be through these centuries
If you let me deep into your mind
I will clean your imagination be it rusty
Since you've kept me shut - all these centuries
If you dare to open my pages and read aloud
You will have redeemed me as your trusty
Old friend The Book, from centuries ago.

The Busker

On the metropolitan concrete
Where you're sitting on the street
You tap away on your bongos
Feel the rhythm of the city's feet
Embrace the sway of the music
Of the dude with the blue guitar
And when there's a congregation
You feel like you're a star
But O' you're only a busker
A small man in the town
But you can play some high music
When the city's blue and down
And you can sing to the rooftops
Or bellow to the underground
Yeah you can hold the people's ear
Wherever you make your sound
So play, play your good music
That you know by mind and heart
And I will drop you a note in
For the gratitude of your art
People may walk by with blinkers
People may dash by at speed
But you take the time to sit and play
Perhaps the world should take heed
But O' you're only a busker
An unusual sort of guy
Perhaps you have a sad story
Behind the smiling of your eyes
But when you sing to the city
You've made another guy smile
And perhaps that bit of money
Will help you out for a while

On the metropolitan concrete
Where you're sitting on the street
You look immersed in your music
This is when your soul is complete.

A Toad in the Road

And the old lorry driver stopped in the road,
Jumped down from his high cab and said to the toad,
'Oh toad will you hobble on so you can pass,
To the safest toad highway on that green bank of grass',
The toad stared at the driver with blinking black eyes,
Said the man to the creature, 'You do look surprised,
But I've done you a favour so waddle on by,
And never again cross this road - you could die',
So the toad lumbered on and the driver stood near,
Making sure that the little toad's path was quite clear,
And the old lorry driver hopped back to his place,
As he rubbed his cold hands a glad smile crossed his face,
For he knew he had done a kind deed for the toad,
'Though the toad couldn't help *him* back over the road,
And a good few years later when the man was quite frail,
He sat slumped in his garden like a trodden down snail,
With a palette of paints and a canvas so white,
That it dazzled his eyes with the glare of sunlight,
Dressed in moth-eaten clothes and one battered old shoe,
He had bones stiff with boredom and nothing to do,
With his paintbrush quite dry and his heart filled with hate,
He saw a little brown toad crawl under his gate,
So he said to the toad, 'You sit there on that stone',
And then the old man didn't feel so alone,
And with a few strokes of the toad on his seat,
The man knew his white canvas would now be complete.

An Autumn Walk on his Local Beach

And his face held the shadow of the long autumn day
That slipped behind the houses that surrounded the bay
And each house lit its lamps in each room of each home
But his stood separate from the others, dark, silent and alone
And he walked by the sea on the pebble-rife sand
And turned over the ring that he held in his hand
And he walked, thought and wandered, just as he'd planned
Until a stranger approached him over the sand
And greeted him warmly in the cool autumn night
For she held a lantern that blessed him with sight
And lit up the sea as a rough shard of glass
That lit up the future as well as the past
For the night had drawn in so fast over the sea
That he had not realised he could not see
Where he was walking, that he was alone
Or that he had wandered so far from his home
Because he was in danger from the incoming storm
But the stranger, she hadn't just approached him to warn
And so they went walking on back to the town
But his face was still haunted by the ghost of a frown
So she asked him his troubles and he told her a few
And gently, she nodded and began to construe
Why he was walking, why he was alone
And she reached out her hand now to help lead him home
And she took him to her wood shack on the edge of the sea
But he still wasn't sure who this lady could be
Perhaps she was an angel, or a winter's-eve ghost
Although this wasn't really what mattered the most
For they sat and they talked in her humble abode
And they sat there 'til morning; for he couldn't go
Back on his own now, out into the cold
For he'd touched on something that felt like raw gold

And they sat and they talked and they laughed and they sang
Until the old doorbell then pitifully rang
And there on the doorstep with no address and no name
A parcel with no sender in the long autumn rain
Who had delivered it? Who was it from?
But the mystery sender had evidently gone
And the lady, she said it was a parcel for him
And she led him outside in the stormy sea wind
And they walked in the rain to the edge of the sand
And stood with the parcel his hand in her hand
And although they were soaking, their faces were warm
For they felt something special had arrived with the dawn
So he opened the parcel and smiled in great awe
And he kissed her; he wasn't alone anymore
And his face held the tears of the long autumn rain
But they were no longer tears of sadness or pain
Down their faces fell tears that showered to the ground
And ran together down the sand, to the sea, they were bound.

Terra Nova Return

Ragged haggard shreds of men
Driving on, driving through
Through the front of roaring white
Hands and faces sunken blue
Trudging trekking on for miles
Eight-hundred miles, with spirits damp
Across the sheets of glaring ice
In desperate bid to reach the camp
A return trip from their losing race
The fungus of failure frothing hot
For Amundsen's team had got there first
At three weeks late Scott's team had not
Descending down a glacier
White and limp as a flake of snow
The man in charge of tent and sled
Was first to fall, the first to go
Hunger tearing at their insides
Frostbite blackening each finger
Exhaustion ripping at their muscles
They pressed on; no time to linger
After pitching tent that night
Captain Oates said his line
He declared, "I am just going outside
And I may be some time"
A heroic deed of self-sacrifice
Oates knew that if he went
He wouldn't slow the others down
When he walked out the tent
And twenty miles of struggling on
Eyes scarred with snow blindness
The men had to pitch up tent again;
A blizzard halted their progress

So nine long days sat in the tent
With storms raging outside
The food supplies slowly ran out
Scott's two companions died
No food, no light, no source of warmth
No hope and no great plan
Scott was alone in the wilderness
The loneliest place known to man
Far from home with frozen heart
Scott knew it was his turn
His final expedition
Terra Nova - no return.

A Character I Created

A character I created seeped into life,
He didn't 'spring' he seeped - he developed,
Into reality he crept, limb by limb and thought by...
Thoughts that slunk into my dreams and resonated,
Into the next day (and the next) and haunted my subconscious,
The character I dreamt of was created by me but...
Grew in his own independent and self-determining
fashion,
Until one day I met him in the waking world,
Of reality and sanity,
But life as I knew it (from this moment) was no longer sane,
It was insanely surreal, for my character existed,
He existed.
In every shred, fibre and complexity,
Exactly the way I had imagined him,
Or had he 'imagined himself' in my own fertile mind?
Somehow he seeped into life and stayed there,
Solid and human as every other person I have met,
Yet so peculiarly resoundingly familiar to me,

I talked to him some days, he talked with me,
But he didn't seem to remember,
That he was merely a figment of my imagination,
When others talked to him too I realised,
He was no longer mine,
He was flesh and blood and thought,
He was his own being,
But perhaps he had been all along,
It was just chance that this character, this person,
Was a bubbling life-form - my personified invention,
A character I created seeped into life,
Yet he was born before I set foot on this planet,
He led his own life independent of my thought processes,
But in my heart I felt that he was conceived in my dreams,
For he had not needed to tell me his name,
Or his favourite colour because (of course):
I knew every nuance of his heart and soul.

Don't Worry, My Dear

For now I'm as tough as the hide on my feet
You've left me alone for too long a year
I've learnt how to reap the grain and the wheat
From the dirt and the grime of this city, my dear
My nails are a-blackened with riverside sludge
You've left me alone in the dark end of town
My boots are worn through from each day that I trudge
In this dress I once called my new wedding gown
My eyes are rimmed-red with the tears that have flowed
You've left me alone in more ways than one
The flakes have been colder each winter it's snowed
And the smog has been greener since you've been gone
There are holes in my pockets of your old winter coat
You've left me alone in a city of thieves
Where I have no drawbridge or protective moat
I cannot just sleep with my tired mind at ease
As I wander alone in the shadows I fear
I'm vulnerable here as a woman on the street
You've left me alone, but don't worry, my dear
For now I'm as tough as the hide on my feet.

Living in Memories

The wind's sweet salty taste
Biting my lips once again
I came here years before
But now it's not the same

Maybe you're not here
Or perhaps you are in some way
Still standing on that cliff
Eternal in your last day

So I come searching to the sea
With the hope I'll find you there
Because you never came back home
To wash the sea salt from your hair

Chalk steps where I held your hand
As we climbed down to the bay
But those steps were so old
Those steps wouldn't hold
With your feet so brash and bold
You lost your way

The falling amber star
Casts her blood upon the sea
That shivers with the night
Who snakes cold hands round me

In the same way long ago
Your arms would gently wrap around
And I'd press myself so close
I'd hear and feel your heart pound

Now only seabirds fly
This dark evening by the coast
I didn't think that I would cry
But living in memories hurts the most

I lie down on the edge
And the sharp grass stings my skin
But memories touch my heart
Memories grip my heart
And my eyes now see the stars
With your spirit in

The wind's sweet salty breath
Lets your ghost dance once again
And though it hurts to remember
I'm truly glad I came
Glad I came.

Married Strangers

Do you trust me still, my dear?
Since the East has cast me out
You've worn a stranger's eye
And your lips are curved with doubt
We met inside the kitchen dark
Cold flagstones, draughty vent
And stood a wall where old embrace
Lingered like stale scent
You're stiffer and more tentative
Creased fingers don't reach out
You're kneading bread belligerently
Withdrawn in sullen pout

Your face is scrawled with wrinkles
Grey eyes a veil of ice
Did you laugh at all while I was gone?
Did you think about me twice?
Is your oily bun scraped tighter?
Or is it the murky light
Hindering my memories
Twisting watered sight?
Are you not still the milky broth
That you used to be?
Is that why you breathe abhorrence,
Or is it the sight of me?

A Telegram, of Sorts, for You

I love you.
And I write you this
With words that are winged;
And now fly to you
Like delicate inky birds
Soaring towards your eyes
From this aromatic brown paper
They set fire to your brain
And touch your heart.
For there is magic in us all
But within you
Are the same inherent wonders
Lying within me
And this telegram of sorts
Is a way of reaching you
Without you even knowing
That these words are a message
Destined for your mind

And so I hope you will realise
One day perhaps
On the pebbled southern beaches
Or the wild western moors
Perhaps watching the stars one night
When I too am watching
And although we may be roads or towns or cities apart
These magic sky-borne embers
Bring us together
As we stare at the same object
In unison
And regard its beauty
Just as I once saw you
And you too, perhaps, saw me
And these winged words
Fly like stars
To your lips
And kiss them
Telling you softly
That I do love you
And always have.

A House or a Home

Even after you've packed up
Driven to the new house
And the brown boxes are emptied of their contents
Even after you've received your 'moving-in' cards
And your status cries, "I've moved in y'all"
You haven't really
Because all you know
Is your old house
(which is still your home)
The memories live there
Even if you don't
(Officially)
And the stains in the carpet
From your brother's ketchup accident
And the scars on the wallpaper
From each night you kicked it in your sleep
And the rips in the curtains
From the time your sister
Tried to cut the "money" out of the lining
Tell the stories of the house's true inhabitants
Which are not the people that have bought it
But you and your loving parents
And your mad brother and sister
(And the fish perhaps)
And things, bizarrely, stay this way
Until years and years
Later.
Years and years
That pass like the cobbles
Rushing under your feet
Blurred in your peripheral vision
As you stride

For the thousandth time
Down that 'stranger's' garden path
Towards a front door you actually
Recognise As Your Own.
And you sit
- in a habitual way -
With your back against the wall
And your bottom in the carpet
And this feels natural
But your mind wanders
And you try to recall the house
That house of before
And parts slip from your memory
Features hide in grey shadows
And you can smell the memory
Of the scent of *that* house
In your nostrils
Because it is a stranger's smell now
The house you sit in seems to have no smell
But of course it does
For the smell is yours
The house you sit in is yours
And you are a stranger
To that old house
You loved
And marked with your love
In your childhood
And used to call home.

BEING HUMAN

What is Poetry?

Poetry is an expulsion of hate
A bubbling toxin that burns up the page
A means of venting and purifying
Jumbled thoughts that need clarifying
A beacon of light from deep within
With colours reflecting the mood one's in
A tornado of vowels and harsh consonants
A splatter of insults and compliments
Sharp shapes formed with words of rage
Vicious lines scrawled on innocent page
A venomous poison of all that we think
A bitter fire burning, in the blues of sad ink
Emotions convulsed up from deep within
An unveiling of troubles, conflicts and sin
A piece to be read and understood
A piece to make you feel sad or good
Poetry is discharge of feelings pent up tight
It is hate, anger, greed, loss
And the pure desire to write.

Black-Veiled Spell

Eyes see a story etched on the canvas of a black veil
An untouchable dimension we can only visit in our mind
Sometimes we know it's a façade, when we visit
But we sometimes believe.
And when one trusts in this paralysed adventure
It becomes so real that it's irrationally beautiful
Or scary, when one cannot escape
From the entombment of their self-made creations
And to shake this drugged paralysis
One's limbs twitch involuntarily
Eyes move wildly behind the black veil
Lungs gasp and voice screams silently
Until the lips break into this world with a wail
And they shake the heavy cover of night
And daylight pierces and enters
Their eyes that embrace reality
And the black-veiled spell is broken
All imaginings fly free.

Words Are Like Knives

Words are like knives
Embedding deep
Into old wounds
Memories keep
Words are like knives
Inflicting pain
Leaving ugly
Crimson stains
Words are like knives

Often banned
Often deadly
In the wrong hands
Words are like knives
Fearful power
That twists the sweet
Into the sour
Words are like knives
They cause awful defects
But when used for good
They can also protect
Words are like knives
When they get wings
They can carve out
Beautiful things.

The Ring of Life

Splattered with blood rubies
Their fearsome eyes deep and bold
Set with cold cut crystal
Upon a satin wreath of gold
A ring of life upon warm flesh
Set with strange and foreign stones
Sharp sugars of sweet splendour
Of prejudiced, unfamiliar tones
But around the fearful pulsing skin
Is a round and endless hug of gold
The hug of home and memories
The hug of all things dear we hold
In your ring of life, and mine
The closest layer is smooth and strong
Alloyed with kind and glinting smiles
Of that warm place where we belong

We dream that ring will ever fit
And precious gold will not wear thin
For without that hug around one's soul
Those frozen jewels will scratch our skin
Yet some may yearn for crystal's spark
Not that satin wreath of gold
But time will teach us to belong
Like the golden ring to our skin when we're old.

Precious Heart

Believe me now my beating heart
You will not crumble in my chest
Evolution's precious work of art
I'll keep you safe beneath my vest
For I'm the keeper of your keys
The watchman in your tower
And I'll fall fighting to my knees
To defend your every beating hour
I'll shield you from each sword and scythe
That dares to piece your tender form
You are the sign that I'm alive
You keep my mind and spirit warm
No stranger may lay hands on you
I'll never let you shrink or swell
I'll only let you feel what's true
And I will learn to treat you well
Believe me now my beating heart
You will not crumble in my chest
Evolution's precious work of art
I know how to love you best.

The Long Race

At the start line my palms were sticky
Fingers shaky
But my mother was there
To put the white bib on my shirt
To rest her hand on my shoulder
As she advised me
How to run the race
With her sweet kind words
That were full of melodic wisdom
And meant a great deal to me
I set off with the thundering pack
Of sweaty, flying bodies
And I even saw
- Through the rush of colour -
My mother
Running along the side lines
Cheering me on in the crowd
With her smile willing me to succeed
In the first stage
Of the long race
But she was soon washed away
In the raging torrent of spectators
And I could see her no more
And my heart beat heavily
For I knew that she could not
Watch the race
To the end
For I was made a slow runner
So I knew that I wouldn't win
I also knew that I would not stop running
Until the race was through

I would not give in
Because I believed that that was the point
Of the long race
And when I saw the others falling through the finish line
Juxtaposing victory upon tragedy
Waving their arms wildly -
Then dropping them in the slow,
Agonizingly human realisation
That it was suddenly over
And that they wouldn't run again
Because it was The Only Race
And the road was The Only Road
And the long race
Wasn't so long after all,
(As the road itself told me)
And as I neared the finish line
The road reminded me it was old
And had seen many a white shoe
Turn grey on the soul
And I ran, in blurred breath of breeze
Down the road
Around each bend
Towards the end
And the golden finish line
That somewhere behind
In the shade of the evergreen pines
My mother, who it seemed
I'd left so long ago
Waited for me
To return.

Lonely Ocean Liner

A lonely ocean liner
With memories of still water
Chugging on, chugging on
The Pacific sapphire-grey
The lonely ocean liner
Carries cargoes unfamiliar
To an acquainted, yet foreign land
Where waters curl with a different swell
The lonely ocean liner
Cannot cease her progress
Cannot but look ahead
To the horizon orange-blue
The lonely ocean liner
Must ride the haunting night
Must sail through savage storms
Through monsters' claws and tears
My lonely ocean liner
Tough journeys she has taken
On every salty voyage
She yearns for harbours known.

Today I Dug a Hole

Today I dug a deep, deep hole,
In the hard earth with my spade,
And dug until my face was black,
From all the dirt that I had sprayed,
And now I lie beside the hearth,
And ask the ruby flames,
The reason that I dug that hole,
That did inflict such pains,
And as I stare at their old dance,
And hear their hissed reply,
I contemplate that dark, dark pit,
For nothing else have I.
Perhaps I dug it for the thrill,
Of leaden arms and peeling hands,
Perhaps tomorrow I will fill,
That empty space with yellow sands,
But for now the rug beneath my form,
Is hard and cracked with dirt and grit,
A horrid place to sleep for me,
So all night long, awake, I'll sit,
And when the dawn shines once again,
I'll shyly creep outside,
To see the hole of yesterday,
Deep, black and yawning wide,
A deep, deep hole I'll greet at dawn
A useful thing indeed,
A place to throw the waste or dead,
Or plant a fruit-tree seed,
Perhaps I will close up the hole,
Perhaps I'll let it lie,
To save the digger of my bed,
His peeled hands when I die.

Dear Death

Dear Death, your stealth amazes me,
Your nature's too complex to understand,
Your air of morbid secrecy,
Smells foully of the underhand,
Yet, Dear Death you are so simple too,
So plain and black and bottomless,
An anti-climax through and through,
Put in a gipsy wedding dress,
Dear Death, your malice bewilders me,
As lashing as the blinding rain,
You pour on human hearts, you see,
And flood them deep with angst and pain,
Dear Death, your name is a mystery,
For I dare not speak a word of you,
Why can't our human tongues be free?
Not dodge you in tacit taboo,
Dear Death, Dear Sleep, Expiry Date,
Your synonyms are frequent and strange,
You have the power to forge our fate,
Why hide it with words - it will not change?
Dear Death, you keep your every promise,
When you come you bring finality,
I respect you; you're so true and honest,
You strip raw our human mortality,
But Dear Death, this is no use at all,
For you aren't a being in yourself,
Nor the result of a sin or fall
You're a consequence of failing health,
Or neglect or lack of sanitation,
Or wounds inflicted upon each other,
The bombs we plant in other nations,
The blood we steal from our brothers,

Yet, Dear Death, you are a unity-send,
A fate we'll all share without a doubt,
Yet we know so little about this 'end',
Only that one day we will find out.

The Cosmic Unconsciousness

The cosmic unconsciousness is a pattern
That lines the invisible veins of existence
That is the universe and everything
And flows without resistance
Through the pulsing minds of humans
And the air and plants and earth
It joins the random to make a reason
It joins up death with birth
And the small things that pepper our day to day
Are linked by this phenomenon, it seems
And some of these ways so peculiar
They're concepts we touch in our deepest dreams
The objects and people that connect by chance
Seems like a great coincidence
But beneath this, the cosmic unconsciousness
Is always weaving a pattern of sense
And this is why things fall into place
In the way that all stories should
And like all tales, of life or less
In this way, they are understood
It fixes up the fragmented parts of our lives
Like shoelaces tied end to end
The parts of our lives that otherwise fray
Without the sense the unconsciousness sends.

Shapes that Correlate

Sometimes one meets another human
And they know, with them, they will never
See eye -
To eye
For things don't psychologically correlate
And that's okay.
Sometimes.
And other times one meets another person
And they know they will correlate like
Equilateral triangles together
And this is good.
Always.
And always you hope to find 'your shape'
Because there is always one
Who is extra special
And with them
You feel like
A star.
But a perfect star is only made
Of two similar triangles
That fit wonderfully
Together.
And never fall

Apart.

Comfort

Comfort is a pillow,
Where you can rest you head,
Soak the cotton with your tears,
Before you go to bed,
Comfort is the sunlight,
That feeds each tree and flower,
You know no matter where it is,
It's shining every hour,
Comfort is a cuddle,
Warm breath in your ear,
Gentle arms protect you,
And let you know they're here,
Comfort is a birdsong,
That bathes the morning light,
And your heart in music,
And waves away the night,
Comfort is the voice that says,
"I know things aren't quite fine,
The sun's behind the clouds today,
But tomorrow it will shine."

Dear Reader

Dear Reader,
I believe we've met
Because our characters' scenes,
Have entwined themselves,
Many times before,
In our respective shows.
But those times,
Could be long ago,
By the time you read,
These words.
And many scenes may have
Let our intrepid characters
Crawl through them,
And, indeed, we could meet again,
Once these words,
Are on paper.
But one never knows,
When,
Dear Reader,
Or whether,
Dear Friend,
We will meet again before the end
Of the show.
But I hope,
Dear One,
That our scenes will align again,
Not long after,
I have written these words,
And that you might realise,
And reciprocate,
The desire I have,
To know your character's story,

And to share with you the tale of mine,
Not just on occasion,
But for a long,
Long time,
After Heaven has drawn
Her dusty curtains
Over the black night
That hovers above
Our sleeping places
That may or may not
Become one
Before she ends
The show.

Envoi

Buccaneer,
This be a message in a bottle.
The poems on these pages,
Inspired by the intrigue of this planet,
Sealed in a bottle, vintage '98,
Investigate, interpret and entertain
Ideas
In the rhythm of our language,
About how we have made the world,
How the world has made us,
As people
Our emotions, perceptions and relations
As you release the cork and unfurl the withered paper,
You may discover poetry that desires to tug,
At the elusive thread that runs through us all.
To the future,
This is a message about our generation,
To our generation,
Here are *seventy beats,*
Of a heart that belongs
To all of us.

Acknowledgements

Writing is a master of disguising itself as a solitary process. But, in reality, honest writing is the very essence of the world and the people around the one doing the writing. That is why I would like to thank everything and everyone who has been a minute or massive part of my life so far, because without you all these poems would not be, and nor would I.

On an official level, I would like to express my gratitude to a wealth of valuable organisations-

Firstly, thank you to Ocado and Peace One Day for allowing me to publish my winning poem 'Peace One Day' from their competition.

Thank you to Wicked Young Writers for granting me publication of my poem 'Christmas at Granny's' and for running a competition that has both motivated and inspired me to write.

Thank you to the John Clare organisation for consenting to the publication of my poem 'Paradox Landscape', inspired by the work of John Clare.

My enduring thanks to New Writing South for being such a friendly and fantastic team of people who have helped me a great deal with my writing through both workshops and personal support.

Thank you to Chichester Festival Theatre and Joseph Wilde for running a wonderful playwriting programme this year, which I would thoroughly recommend; it has been one of the most worthwhile undertakings of my writing life so far.

And now, my deepest thanks to the individuals who have made this book what it is-

Thank you, Buff and Hugh Eagle for bringing my work to my publisher's attention.

Thank you, Jasper Rolfe, for illustrating the cover of 'Seventy Beats' so beautifully.

Thank you, Kai Bohannon, for the excellent graphic design on the cover.

Thank you, Tony Gordon, for everything; it wouldn't be 'Seventy Beats' without you.

And thank you to all my family; Peter Crundwell for inspiring adventure, Elisabeth Crundwell for being my agent, Natalie Crundwell for being a sister as close as they get, my extended family for your love and constant belief, and particular thanks to Grandpa David, for your delightful commentary on one of the first plays I wrote, dictated to me one summer's afternoon in the garden. Your advice has always encouraged me to better myself.

And thank you, reader, for imagining, immersing, and engaging with the book upon this reading, and I hope you will continue to read it and never stop discovering something new.